FOCKE-WULF Fw 189

By George Punka
Color By Don Greer
& Tom Tullis
Illustrated by Joe Sewell

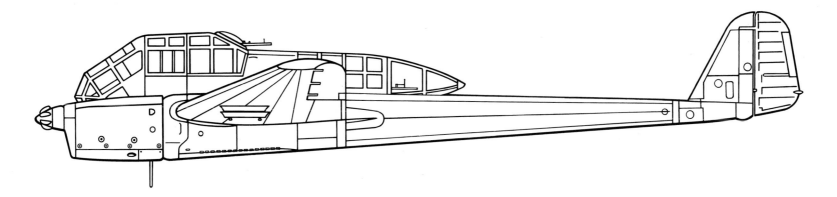

Aircraft Number 142

squadron/signal publications

Joined by a Hungarian Air Force Fw 189A-1, a Luftwaffe Fw-189A-1 makes a reconnaissance flight over the Don River in the Ukraine during 1943. Both aircraft carry the Yellow identification bands carried by Axis aircraft operating on the Eastern Front.

Dedication

The story of Focke Wulf Fw 189, *Fliegende Auge* (Flying Eye) has had little exposure in the written history of the Second World War. This book is intended to tell not only the aircraft's history but to also to provide some information on the crews that flew this wonderful flying machine. I have dedicated this book to Mr. Czigány, Mr. Csapó, Mr. Emmerstorfer, Mr. Fraunhoffer and Mr. Suttay who provided me with information, photographs and their wartime memories. I am also indebted to Mr. Peter Petrick and Mr. Hans-Heiri Stapfer who also assisted me in the preparation of this publication and finally I must thank Mr. Sinka who spent many hours in his darkroom helping with the photos used in this book. Last but not least,I must thank my wife Gyöngyi and my daughter Héidi, who put up with the nearly two years it took to produce this book.

ISBN 0-89747-310-8

If you have any photographs of aircraft, armor, soldiers or ships of any nation, particularly wartime snapshots, why not share them with us and help make Squadron/Signal's books all the more interesting and complete in the future. Any photograph sent to us will be copied and the original returned. The donor will be fully credited for any photos used. Please send them to:

Squadron/Signal Publications, Inc.
1115 Crowley Drive.
Carrollton, TX 75011-5010

Acknowledgments

I must thank the following persons and organizations for the use of their photos, information and for all their assistance in the preparation of this publication:

G. Aders	Dénes Bernád
Attila Bonhardt	Endre Czigány
Béla Csapó	Eddie Creek
Heimo Emmerstorfer	József Fraunhoffer
Robert Gretzynger	Family Andor Gyulay
Volker Koos	Hadtörtenelmi Intezet-Budapest
Richard Lutz	Keski-SuomenIlmailumuseo
Heinz Nowarra	Ferenc Nyakas
Peter Patrick	Willy Radinger
Matti Salonen	András Simorjai
Hans Heiri Stapfer	Matthias Rothe
László Szekely	vitéz János "Koppany" Suttay
Harold Thiele	Mr. Zazvonil
Imre Szalóki	Mr Szentpétery
Ferenc Kovács	

The crew of a Luftwaffe Fw 189A-1 plan their next reconnaissance mission in front of their aircraft somewhere on the Eastern Front. Fw 189s were flown by a crew of three; pilot, radio-operator/gunner and flight mechanic/rear gunner. The port just above the wing was the gun port for one of the two forward firing 7.9mm machine guns.

Introduction

In the February of 1937 the *Technische Amt* (Technical Office) of the *Reichsluftfahrtministerium* (RLM) opened competition for a new aircraft to replace the Luftwaffe's current reconnaissance aircraft that equipped the *Aufklärungsstaffeln* (H) (tactical reconnaissance squadrons) . Up until this time, the Luftwaffe had used the Heinkel He 46 for this role, but this aircraft was rapidly becoming obsolete. The He 46 filled the reconnaissance mission with excellent downward visibility and good slow speed handling. In 1935, Henschel offered the HS 122 as a replacement for the He 46; however, the aircraft was only some six mph (10 km/h) faster than the earlier aircraft. The Hs 122's 167 mph top speed (270 km/h) was deemed to be insufficient and Henschel rebuilt the prototype, using a more powerful engine and improved airframe. This prototype evolved into the Hs 126 high wing, two seat tactical reconnaissance aircraft.

The speed of the prototype was now some 208 mph (335 km/h) with all operational equipment and a full load. This performance was achieved despite its fixed landing gear and strut braced high wing. The aircraft featured an open observer's cockpit which was felt to offer the best field of view for the observer. At the time, the HS 126 was considered to be one of the best all-metal reconnaissance aircraft in service.

The first flight tests of the aircraft were done during the Spanish Civil War in 1938. After these tests, the aircraft entered front-line service with the Luftwaffe. The aircraft had proven to be very suitable for the low level, forward battlefield reconnaissance mission. One drawback with the aircraft was its armament. Defensive armament for the HS 126 consisted of a forward firing MG 15 and a rear mounted MG 15 machine gun in the observer's cockpit. To use the gun, the observer had to store his camera, taking away from his primary task of observation and photographic survey of the battlefield. With its slow speed and poor armament, the HS 126 was an easy target for enemy fighters.

The appearance of fast fighters over the battlefields made the tactic of avoiding air combat all but impossible. It quickly became obvious that a faster and better armed aircraft was needed for the forward reconnaissance role.

The solution to this requirement was the issuing of a new Luftwaffe requirement which called for a crew of three, higher power, increased armament and improved overall performance and the ability to carry a 441 pound (200 kg) bomb load. Three companies undertook initial design studies aimed at this specification; Arado, Blohm Voss and Focke Wulf.

In March of 1937, the three factories began the development work on their designs. The Arado entry emerged as a single engine aircraft with a shoulder mounted wing and enclosed cabin with extensive glazing for good all-around view. Unfortunately the aircraft, the Ar 198, proved to have poor handling characteristics and further development was canceled.

The Blohm Voss aircraft was a single engine, asymmetrical aircraft with the crew housed in a fully-glazed cockpit offset to starboard so that the visibility from the cockpit would not be hampered by the propeller. The *Technische Amt* had little interest in the BV 141 and the firm began the construction of a prototype at their own expenses. In the event, only a limited number of prototype and pre-production aircraft were built and the type never entered front line service.

In April of 1937, Focke Wulf was given a contract for a single prototype under the designation Fw 189. The designer, Kurt Tank, felt that the answer to better performance was through the use of two 450 hp engines which would give the aircraft a total of some 900 hp. The prototype emerged as a twin boomed aircraft with the cabin mounted between the booms. This placed the crew cabin in the clear, in front of the wing, giving the pilot and observer excellent all-round visibility. Although the publication of the official specification by the *Technische Amt* had suggested a single engine design, it was not officially required and it quickly became apparent that the Focke Wulf design had a number of interesting features.

Focke Wulf had planned to use interchangeable fuselage sections so that other roles could be undertaken using the same aircraft, such as training or close support missions. The aircraft was powered by two 465 hp Argus air cooled, inverted-vee engines driving two blade fixed pitch propellers. The twin booms carried the engines and 58 gallon fuel tanks (220 L). The

The prototype Fw 189 V1 in flight over Bremen, Germany during July of 1938. The aircraft was flown on its first flight by its designer, Kurt Tank. The aircraft carried the radio code/registration D-OPVN on the wing in Black. (Emmerstorfer)

booms ended with stressed skin fins and rudders and were joined by a single piece horizontal stabilizer and elevator. The outer wing panels were connected to the booms and were joined to the center wing box by three wing spars. The fully retractable landing gear was hydraulically operated and the tail wheel was also retractable, folding to starboard to lay flat on the under-surface of the horizontal tail plane. The first prototype (registered D-OPVN) made its maiden flight, piloted by Kurt Tank, in July of 1938, some fifteen months after the contract was let.

By the end of 1938, the first prototype (Fw 189 V1) had been joined by two others (Fw 189 V2 [registered D-OVHD] in August and the and Fw 189 V3 {registered D-ORMH} in September). The Fw 189 V2 was basically similar to the FW 189 V1 but was equipped for armament trials with an armament of three 7.9MM MG 15 machine guns. One gun was mounted in the front of the cabin, another was mounted in a flexible position above the cabin and was fired by the wireless operator. The third gun was mounted in the conical rear gunner's position. Additionally, there were two fixed 7.9MM MG 17 machine guns mounted in wing roots and fired by the pilot.

The third prototype (Werk Nr.1999) featured automatic variable-pitch Argus propellers in place of the fixed pitch propellers used on the earlier prototypes and production (also known as Standard) As 410 engines.

The successful outcome of the flight test program with the three prototypes resulted in an order for four additional prototypes. The first of this series, the Fw 189 V4 (D-OCHO-Werk Nr.0001) was the first model of the planned series production Fw 189A. The machine had some minor changes such as modified engine cowlings, semi-cowled main wheels, an enlarged tail wheel and the defensive armament was restricted to a pair of MG 15 machine guns. This aircraft was used to conduct a number of trials with special equipment, such as the Type S 125 smoke-screen equipment and spray containers for spreading poison gas and other chemical warfare agents.

The next aircraft, the Fw l 89 V5, was the first model of the intended Fw 189B series trainer with an aerodynamically refined fuselage nacelle. The original fuselage was replaced by a heavy armored cockpit for the pilot and rear gunner. The pilot was seated back to back with the gunner.

The third prototype was originally registered D-ORMH before being given the Luftwaffe radio call sign GJ+RT. The Fw 189 V3 featured a single leg main landing gear and was powered by Standard As 410 engines with variable pitch propellers. (Emmerstorfer)

The second prototype was designated the Fw 189 V2 and given the registration D-OVHD. The V 2 prototype was similar to the Fw 189 V1 but was equipped with armament for armament trials. The two items under the wing above the (-) are bomb racks. (Hans-Heiri Stapfer)

At the end of 1939, the Fw 189 Vl had been pulled out of the flight testing and had been converted for the assault or close-support role under the designation Fw 189 V1b. The original nacelle was replaced by an small armored nacelle where the pilot and gunner sat back to back. The pilot was protected by armor glass panels and sat in an armored seat. The gunner's seat was also armored and he was provided with a single 7.9MM MG 15 machine gun.. Later, another prototype of the assault variant was built under the designation Fw 189 V6. This new model was intended to be the prototype for the series production the Fw 189C.

The last prototype was ordered as a seaplane. This variant, the Fw 189 V7, employed a similar fuselage and wings to the Fw 189 V5, but was configured with twin floats. This aircraft was not finished and was later converted to the Fw 189D configuration.

At one point, a radial type engine variation had been planned which was to have been powered by a pair of 700 hp Gnome Rhone 14M 4/5 fourteen cylinder air cooled radial engines . One Fw 189A-1 airframe was converted to take these engines at Chatillon-sur-Seine by SNCASO. The aircraft was proposed for production under the designation Fw 189E; however, the prototype crashed while being ferried to Germany for evaluation during early 1943 and the program was scrapped. After repairs, the prototype was given the registration GI+RO and was taken for Fieldmarshal Kesselring as his personal courier aircraft entering service in May of 1943.

The Fw 189 V1 prototype was rebuilt with an entirely armored fuselage as the prototype for an armored assault/close support variant of the Fw 189 with the designation Fw 189 V1b. The aircraft was later lost during a demonstration in early 1943.

Development

Fw 189 V1
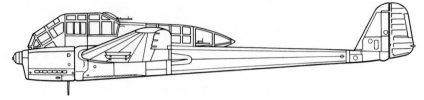

Fw 189 V2
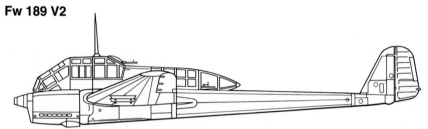

Fw 189 V4
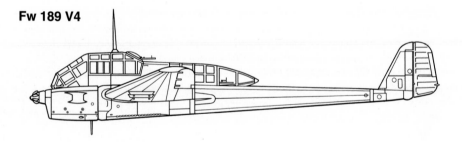

Fw 189 V1b
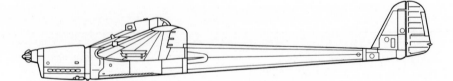

Fw 189 V6
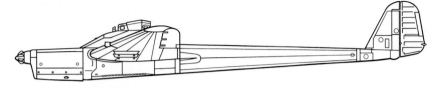

Fw 189A-1/2
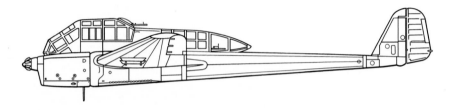

Fw 189B
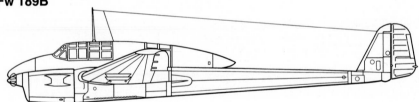

Fw 189 Nightfighter
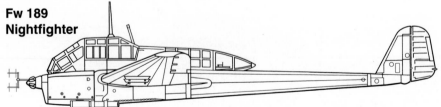

Focke Wulf Fw I89A

During the Spring of 1940, Focke Wulf received production orders for ten pre-production Fw 189A-0s, to be followed by twenty production Fw 189A-1s. The Fw 189A-1 was basically similar to the Fw 189V4 prototype with some additional aerodynamic refinement of the engine cowlings and a twin leg main undercarriage. Armament was standardized at a pair of forward firing MG 17s and two flexible MG 15 machine guns, one for the observer and a second gun for the rear gunner. Additionally, four ETC 50/VIII bomb racks were installed under the outboard wing panels capable of carrying four 154 pound (70 kg) SC 50 bombs. The GV 219d bomb sight could be used for both horizontal and dive bombing. The aircraft was also equipped to carry the S 125 *Rauchbehalter* smoke generator. Normal reconnaissance equipment was one RB 20/30 camera. Other optional installations included the RB 50/30, RB 21/18 or the R.R 15/18 cameras. The crew also had a Type HK 12.5 or HK 19 hand-held camera. Normally, an FUG 25 radio was installed along with a G4 type compass. For night reconnaissance, the aircraft could carry photoflash bombs. The crew of the Fw 189A-1 was comprised of a pilot, observer-navigator/radio-operator/dorsal gunner and the flight mechanic/rear gunner.

The ten pre-production and twenty production aircraft were built all in the company's facility in Bremen, Germany. The service evaluation of the pre-production Fw 189A-0 reconnais-

Fw 189As under varying stages of construction at the Focke Wulf plant in Bremen, Germany. Behind the aircraft in the foreground are rows of completed center fuselage sections. (Emmerstorfer)

An Fw 189A (Wr.Nr.0046) just off the assembly line and ready for painting. Even though the aircraft is still overall Natural Metal, a single Black cross has been painted on the starboard wing uppersurface. (Emmerstorfer)

sance aircraft was progressing and reports on the aircraft were excellent. The *Oberkommamdo der Luftwaffe* (OKL) had finally realized that the HS 126 had reached the end of its usefulness and assigned the Fw l89A program a high priority and a second assembly line was established at the Aero-Avia factory in Czechoslovakia. One reason for this switch

An Fw 189A-1 (Wr. Nr. 0032) undergoes final assembly in the Focke Wulf plant in Bremen, Germany. The engine cowlings for the Argus As 410 air cooled engines are open for final checks of the aircraft's power plants. The Fw 89A-1 differed from the Fw 189 V4 in that it featured a twin leg main landing gear for additional strength. (Emmerstorfer)

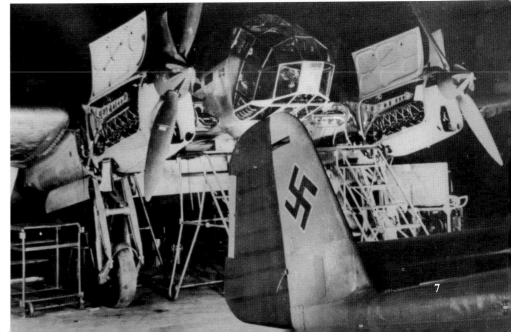

was because the assembly lines in Bremen were taken over with production of the Fw 190 fighter.

By late Summer of 1940, the factory of Bremen had handed over thirty-eight Fw 189s to the Luftwaffe and during 1941 a further sixty-one Fw 189A-1s were produced. During this time period, the Aero works delivered 151 machines to the Luftwaffe and towards the end of the year, component parts were being delivered from Bremen to captured aircraft factories in Bordeaux, France so that production of the Fw 189A could begin at this location. The final assembly of German supplied sub-assemblies was carried out at work shops at Merignac.

By the Spring of 1942, substantial numbers of Fw 189As had arrived to re-equip operational *Aufklärungsstaffeln* (H) reconnaissance units in the field. The priority for re-equipment was for units serving on the Eastern Front (where the Fw 189 was to see most of its service).

During 1942, the factory at Bremen built a total of fifty-seven aircraft, the Aero-Avia works produced 183 aircraft and the factory of Bordeaux turned out some eighty-seven aircraft. By the Spring of 1943, the French group of factories had taken over the production of the Fw 189 from the factory at Bremen with the German and Czech factories phasing out production (eleven aircraft built at Bremen and three at Prague).

During mid-1941, production was shifted from the Fw 189A-1 to the Fw 89A-2. The only external difference between the two variants was the armament. The Fw 189A-2 differed only in having strengthened defensive weapons. The single MG 15 machine guns were replaces by MG 81Z (twin MG 81 guns). These machine guns had a rate of fire of some 3,600 rounds per minute.

...The Fw 189A-3 was a dual-control pilot trainer built in small numbers alongside the Fw 189A-2. The final A series variant was the Fw 189A-4 which differed from the earlier versions in having the wing root machine guns replaced with MG FF 20mm cannon. Additionally, light armor was added beneath the engines, fuselage and fuel tanks for the low level tactical reconnaissance and close support role.

Pairs of 465 hp Argus AS 410 air-cooled, inverted Vee engines rest on transport dollies ready for installation on completed Fw 189A-1 airframes at the Focke Wulf plant in Bremen, Germany.

An Fw 189A-1 awaits attachment of the outer wing panels on the Focke Wulf assembly line. The elevator and rudders on the Fw 189 were fabric covered, as were the ailerons on the outer wing panels. (Emmerstorfer)

Cowling Development

Fw 189 V1

Fw 189 V4

Fw 189A-1

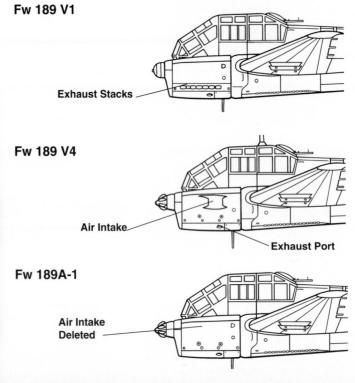

Exhaust Stacks

Air Intake

Exhaust Port

Air Intake Deleted

The cowling on the Fw 189A-1 differed from the Fw 189 V4 prototype in that it deleted the air intake on the side of the cowling, improving overall aerodynamics. The exhausts were changed from individual stacks used on the Fw 189 V1 to an exhaust collector with a single exhaust port on the lower portion of each side of the cowling. (Emmerstorfer)

The twelve cylinder Argus engines drove Argus two blade, controllable pitch propellers. The vaned propeller hub was the pitch control for the propeller. The landing gear differed from the prototypes in that it was a twin leg rather than single leg design. (Emmerstorfer)

The Fw 1879A-1 had two MG 15 7.9mm machine guns as defensive armament. One gun was carried in the dorsal turret and fired by the observer while the second was in the tail cone and was fired by the engineer/rear gunner. (Hans-Heiri Stapfer)

An early production Fw 189A-1 on the ramp at the Focke Wulf plant during 1941. The aircraft carried the Luftwaffe radio code SI+EM on each boom and under the wing. The gun in the upper turret was a 7.9mm MG 15. (Emmerstorfer)

9

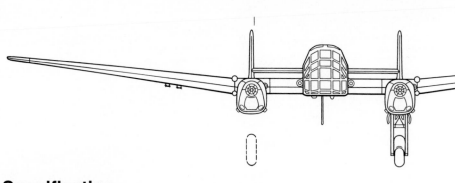

Specification

Focke Wulf Fw 189A-1

Wingspan...60 feet 4.5 inches (18.44 m)
Length..39 feet 5.5 inches (12 m)
Height..10 feet 2 inches (3.12 m)
Empty Weight...6.239 pounds (2,830 kg)
Maximum Weight....................................9,193 pounds (4,169 kg)

Powerplant...Two 465 hp Argus
                                                                   As 410A-1 air cooled engines
Armament...Two forward firing MG 17 7.9mm
                                                                   machine guns, one MG 15 upper turret
                                                                   machine gun and one MG 15 in rear turret.
Speed...217 mph (349.2kph)
Service Ceiling.......................................23,950 feet (7,299.9 m)
Range...416 miles (669.4 km)
Crew...Three

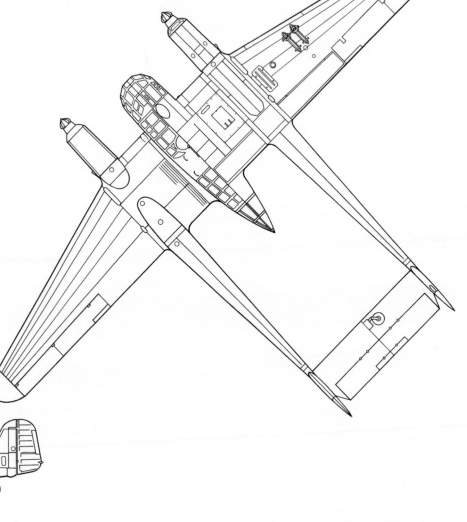

The two small air intakes on either side of the large center cooling air intake were used to feed cooling air for the oil cooler. Besides these main intakes, there was a smaller air intake mounted on the cowling just in front of the wing. The engine cowling had two large upward hinged servicing panels on either side of the cowl that allowed easy access to the entire engine. The view forward and downward for the pilot was excellent. (Hans-Heiri Stapfer)

(Right) Luftwaffe ground crewmen load 110 pound (50 kg) SC 50 general purpose bombs onto one of the ETC 50/VIII underwing bomb racks of a Fw 189A-1. The Fw 189 could carry a four such bombs for a total bomb load of 440 pounds. Normally, the Fw 189 was used for visual/photographic reconnaissance missions and was rarely used for bombing missions. Aircraft on the Eastern Front; however, were used for missions against Russian Partisans, bombing supply dumps, base camps and personnel whenever they were caught in the open.

Four early production Fw 189A-1s on the factory ramp prior to acceptance tests. The aircraft in the foreground carries the Luftwaffe radio code GI+RG on the tail boom in Black. None of these aircraft have their armament fitted. (Hans-Heiri Stapfer)

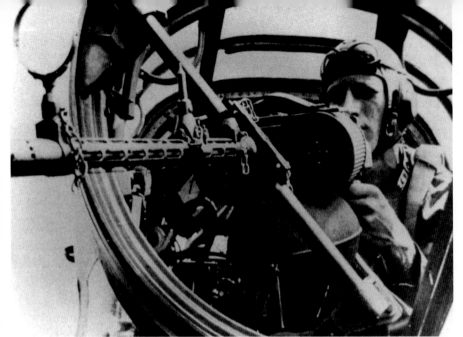

The Fw 189A-1 was armed with a single 7.9MM MG 17 machine gun in the tail cone. The weapon was fed from drum magazines that could be quickly changed in flight. There were racks for spare magazines alongside the gunner and in the fuselage below the top turret.

Experience in combat with the Fw 189A-1 led to an increase in the defensive armament on the Fw 189A-2. The rear gunner's position was modified with a MG 81Z twin 7.9MM machine gun being installed in place of the earlier single MG 17 installation.

The rubber bag under the MG 15 machine gun is to collect the shell casings. The glasses on the gunner's head were known as *Splitterschutzbrille* glasses and were intended to protect the gunner from both glass splinters in the event of a hit on the turret. They were tinted to also serve as sun glasses. (Sinka)

This Fw 189A-2 has belt fed instead of the more usual drum fed MG 81Z twin 7.9MM machine gun installation in the tail cone. There is a shell casing ejection chute installed under the fuselage just forward of the turret.

Tail Turrets

Fw 189A-1

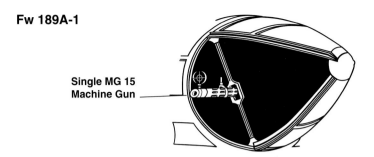

Single MG 15
Machine Gun

Fw 189A-2

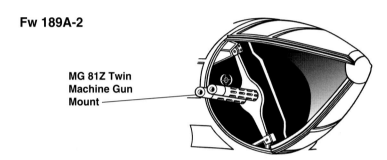

MG 81Z Twin
Machine Gun
Mount

Fw 189A-1s and early Fw 189A-2s had a single 7.9мм MG 17 installed in the dorsal turret. Both drum fed and belt fed guns were used and a variety of gun sights were fitted. (Hans-Heiri Stapfer)

Late Fw 189A-2s were fitted with an armor glass turret with a MG 81Z twin 7.9мм machine gun installation. This was a common installation on aircraft serving on the Eastern Front. (Thiele)

Dorsal Turrets

Fw 189A-1

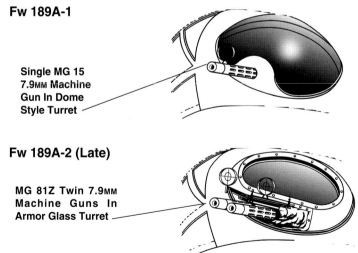

Single MG 15
7.9мм Machine
Gun In Dome
Style Turret

Fw 189A-2 (Late)

MG 81Z Twin 7.9мм
Machine Guns In
Armor Glass Turret

Focke Wulf Fw 189B

The Fw 189 V5 prototype, was intended to serve as the test vehicle for the planned Fw 189B trainer series. This variant differed from the Fw 189A in that it had a new fuselage with dual controls. With its primary role of training, the Fw 189B had all its armament deleted. After the completion of test flying with the Fw 189 V5, the three-production Fw 190B-0s were ordered along with ten production Fw 189B-1 trainers. All of the five seat aircraft were completed during early 1940 and delivered to the Luftwaffe units.

The role of machines was originally intended to be night fighting and wireless operator training, and the inside the fuselage was packed with instruments and radio panels for each student crew position. All Fw 189Bs were powered by the Standard Argus As 410 engines driving automatic variable-pitch propellers. Later, most of the aircraft were modified with a reinforced main undercarriage. A number of the aircraft were used in the courier roles and, from time to time, were used as VIP aircraft for high ranking Luftwaffe personnel.

(Right) This was one of the early pre-production Fw 189B-0 with an early engine installation without the side air intakes. The aircraft had the Luftwaffe radio codes, BQ+AZ on the tail booms in Black.There were only three Fw 189B-0s built (Nowarra)

This Fw 189B-1 was assigned to a training squadron and carried an overall Gray camouflage with the radio codes, BS+AA in Black. This is an early Fw 189B-1with the single leg main landing gear. Besides its training role, the Fw 189B also served as a liaison and VIP aircraft for high ranking Luftwaffe officials. (Emmerstorfer)

Fuselage Development

Fw 189A-1

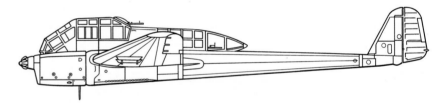

Fw 189B-1

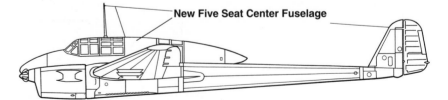

New Five Seat Center Fuselage

Focke Wulf Fw 189C

Late in 1938, the Fw 189 Vl was returned to the company work shop for conversion to the close support/assault role. The aircraft had the original fuselage removed and replaced by an entirely new small two man armored center fuselage with increased armor plating and heavier armament. The prototype was re-designated the Fw 189 V1b and began flight testing in the Spring of 1939. Flight tests soon revealed that the handling characteristics were unsatisfactory, the take-off weight had increased dramatically and the forward vision through the small armor glass panels was bad. Additionally, the gunner had difficulty in seeing an aircraft behind the Fw 189 V1b. As a result, the aircraft was returned to the factory for modification.

The cockpit armor glass panels were enlarged, the rear visor for the gunner was replaced by an armored enclosure with additional view panels. After these modifications, the Fw 189 Vlb, was given a new registration and radio code NA+BW. The aircraft was used to undertake comparative trials with the assault/close support Henschel Hs 129. The results of these trials were inconclusive, since the flight qualities of Focke Wulf were no better like the Hs 129. Shortly after the trials, the Fw 189 Vlb was lost during a demonstration at Bremen. The accident was caused by a near collision with a building during landing. The pilot was injured in the resulting belly landing and the aircraft was written off.

Interestingly, the Fw 189 Vlb had gained some support from Luftwaffe officials and as a result another prototype, the Fw 189V6 (registered D-OPVN), was constructed to serve as the prototype for the proposed Fw 189 C assault/close-support aircraft. This prototype was completed in early 1940. The Fw 189V6 central fuselage nacelle was similar to the proposed pro-

Focke Wulf technicians work on the Fw 189 V6 prototype in the Focke Wulf factory in Bremen, Germany, during 1940. The Fw 189 V6 was intended to serve as the prototype for the Fw 189C assault/close support variant. The aircraft did not go into series production, mainly due to its high costs. (Emmerstorfer)

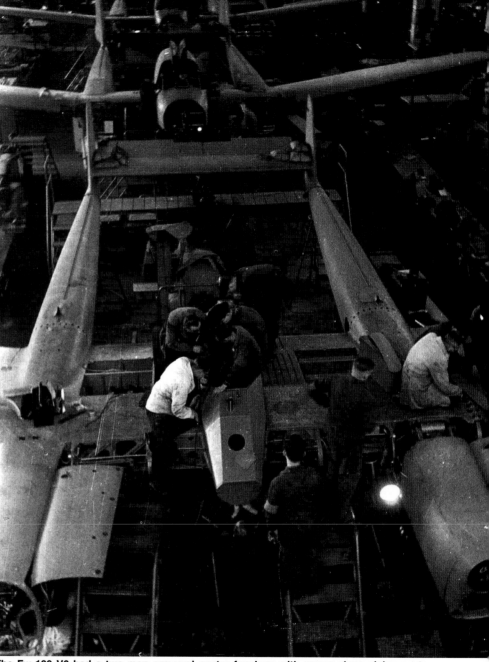

The Fw 189 V6 had a two man armored center fuselage with armor glass vision ports. The aircraft was armed with two forward firing 20MM MG FF cannon and four forward firing 7.9MM MG 17 machine guns mounted in the wing center section. The gunner's position had a MG 81Z twin 7.9MM flexible machine gun mount. The aircraft in the background are Fw 189B trainers.

The Fw 189 V6 was registered D-OPVN and carried the civil registration on the tail boom and wing undersurfaces in Black. Later the single leg main landing gear was replaced with a twin leg landing gear. (Kovács)

duction nacelle, the aircraft was powered by the 465 hp Argus As 41OA-1 engines, had a strengthened main undercarriage with twin oleo legs and a new strengthened wing center section for the new armored fuselage. This center wing panel housed two 20MM MG FF cannon and four 7.9MM MG 17 machine guns. The gunner's position had a pair of 7.9MM MG 81 flexible machine guns and improved vision blocks.

After the testing by *5 (Schlacht) Staffel of Lehrgeschwader 2*, service pilots appeared to favor the Fw 189C, while being opposed to the competing Hs 129A-0 which most found to be

The Fw 189 V6 was tested with chemical spray containers mounted on the underwing ETC 50/VIII bomb racks. It was intended that these containers would be used to carry poison gas and other chemical warfare agents. (Creek)

totally unacceptable. The RLM; however, felt that due to its much higher costs, the Fw 189C did not show a significant improvement over the Hs 129 and production plans were abandoned.

FUSELAGE DEVELOPMENT

Fw 189 V1b

Two Man Armored Center Fuselage Section

Early Engines
With Individual
Exhaust Stacks

Fw 189 V6

Revised Center Fuselage With Improved
Vision Ports and MG 81Z Rear Turret

Standard Argus
As 410 Engines

In Service

In the Spring of 1940, a number of Fw 189s had been delivered to experimental sections of the Luftwaffe and some of these were attached to several reconnaissance squadrons for service trials. A training unit, *9. (H) Lehrgeschwader 2* received five aircraft to conduct comparison testing between the Fw 189A-O and their Hs 126s .After successful. completion of these trials during the Summer of 1940, the Luftwaffe ordered full production of the Fw 189 A-1 and before the end of the year Focke Wulf had delivered thirty-eight aircraft to the Luftwaffe although these were not assigned to service units.

During 1941, some 250 aircraft had been produced but this was not enough to completely replace the Hs 126 in front line units and when Operation BARBAROSSA, the invasion of the Soviet Union, began on 22 July 1942, most front line short-range reconnaissance squadrons still flew Hs 126s. At the time of the attack, the Luftwaffe short-range reconnaissance units were deployed with *Heeresgruppe* (Army Group) *Mitte* (Middle), *Nord* (North) and *Sud* (South) as follows:

Unit	Area	Unit	Area
1.(H)10	Heeresgruppe Mitte	1.(H)13Pz	Heeresgruppe Mitte
2.(H)10	Heeresgruppe Mitte	2.(H)13	Heeresgruppe Nord
4.(H)10	Heeresgruppe Nord	3.(H)13	Heeresgruppe Sud
		4.(H)13	Heeresgruppe Sud
1.(H)11	Heeresgruppe Mitte	5.(H)13	Heeresgruppe Sud
5.(H)11Pz	Heeresgruppe Sud	6.(H)13Pz	Heeresgruppe Mitte
		7.(H)13	Heeresgruppe Mitte
1.(H)12	Heeresgruppe Nord		
2.(H)12	Heeresgruppe Mitte	1.(H)14	Heeresgruppe Sud
3.(H)12	Heeresgruppe Mitte	3.(H)14	Heeresgruppe Mitte
4.(H)12	Heeresgruppe Mitte	5.(H)14Pz	Heeresgruppe Sud
5.(H)12	Heeresgruppe Mitte		
6.(H)12	Heeresgruppe Sud	9.(H)LG2	Heeresgruppe Mitte
7.(H)12	Heeresgruppe Mitte		
1.(H)21	Heeresgruppe Mitte	1.(H)32	Eismeer Front
2.(H)21	Heeresgruppe Nord	2.(H)32	Heeresgruppe Mitte
3.(H)21	Heeresgruppe Sud	3.(H)32	Heeresgruppe Sud
4.(H)21	Heeresgruppe Nord	4.(H)3.2	Heeresgruppe Sud
5.(H)21	Heeresgruppe Sud	5.(H)32	Heeresgruppe Sud
6.(H)21	Heeresgruppe Sud	6.(H)32	Heeresgruppe Mitte
7.(H)21	Heeresgruppe Nord	7.(H)32	Heeresgruppe Mitte
		8.(H)32	Heeresgruppe Sud
1.(H)23	Heeresgruppe Sud		
2.(H)23	Heeresgruppe Nord		
3.(H)23Pz	Heeresgruppe Nord	1.(H)41	Heeresgruppe Sud
4.(H)23	Heeresgruppe Nord	2.(H)41	Heeresgruppe Mitte
5.(H)23	Heeresgruppe Mitte	3.(H)41	Heeresgruppe Nord
		4.(H)41	Heeresgruppe Su
1.(H)31	Heeresgruppe Mitte	5.(H)41	Heeresgruppe Mitte
2.(H)31	Heeresgruppe Sud	6.(H)4lPz	Heeresgruppe Mitte
4.(H)31	Heeresgruppe Nord		
5.(11)31	Heeresgruppe Sud		
6.(H)31	Heeresgruppe Mitte		

During the Winter of 1941-42 the reconnaissance units of the Luftwaffe were completely reorganized and the short-range reconnaissance squadrons *Aufklaungsstaffeln* (H) were reorganized as short-range reconnaissance groups *Nahaufklörungsgruppen* (NAG). These units were assigned to the ground units and reported directly to the unit commanders. Under this reorganization, sixteen short-range reconnaissance groups were established, although not all were up to their full established strength of three attached squadrons.

By the end of 1941, the Wehrmacht had to assign units for defensive operations because of a lack of adequate reserves and the developing Russian resistance movement. There also were tremendous losses in the short-range reconnaissance units. Numerous squadrons had to be disbanded or reorganized because of a lack of aircraft and personal losses. These terminated squadrons included: 4.(H)21, 5.(H)21, 6.(H)21, 7.(H) 21, 5.(H)31, 6.(H)31 6.(H)12 ,4.(H)22, 3.(H)23, 5. (H)23, 1.(H)14 and 5.(H)14.

The remaining aircraft and crews of terminated squadrons were passed to newly formed units. At the beginning of 1942 the NAG units were as follows:

Units on the southern sector of the Eastern Front

Group	Squadrons
NAG 1	5.(H)11
NAG 4	2.(H)41
	2. (H)13
NAG 6	7. (H)13 (Hs 126)
NAG 7	1.(H)10 (Hs 126)
	4. (H)10 (Hs 126)
NAG 8	4. (H)31
	3.(H)13 (Hs 126)
	4.(H)23 (Hs 126)

Ground crewmen prepare an Fw 189A of 7.(H)32 for a reconnaissance mission in *Heersgruppe Mitte* (Army Group Middle) on the Eastern Front during late 1942. The unit emblem of the cowling was in White.

Group	Squadrons
NAG 9	1.(H)21
	7.(H)32
NAG 10	2.(H)10
NAG 12	6.(H)41
	2.(H)32
NAG 16	3. (H) 12
	5.(11)12 (Hs 126)

Units in the middle sector of the Eastern Front

Group	Squadrons
NAG 2	3.(H)21(Hs 126)
	1.(H)41(Hs 126)
	2.(H)23 (Hs 126)
NAG 5	1.(H)11
	2.(H)12 (Hs 126)
NAG 8	4.(H)23 (Hs 126)
NAG 10	5.(H)32 (Hs 126)
NAG 11	1.(H)31
	2.(H)31
	1.(H)13 (Hs 126)
NAG 15	1.(H)12 (Hs 126)
	6.(H)32 (HS 126)
	2.(H)13

An Fw 189A-1 shares a landing ground with the aircraft it was replacing, the Hs 126 reconnaissance aircraft. The Fw 189 has a protective cover over the glass areas to keep the aircraft's interior from becoming too hot. (Thiele)

Units on the northern sector of the Eastern Front

Group	Squadrons
NAG 13	2.(H)21(Hs 126)
	3.(H)41(Hs 126)

Units on the North Sea Front

Group	Squadron
	1. (H) 32

Africa Corps Units

Group	Squadron
	2.(H)14 (Hs 126)

In December of 1941 the German 9th Army gave up Kalinin and Soviet troops started a counter-attack. Because of the extreme cold, preparing aircraft for missions in the field was extremely difficult and there were shortages of spare parts, fuel and personnel. As a result, the short-range reconnaissance units were once again reorganized with a further reduction of independent squadrons.

Group	Squadrons	Front Sector
NAG 1	5.(H)11	South
NAG 2	1.(H)41	Middle
	2.(H)13	"
	3.(H)21	"
NAG 4	2.(H)41	South
	6.(H)13	"
NAG 6	7.(H)13	"
NAG 7	1.(H)10	"
	4.(H)l0	"

This Fw 189 is not fitted with the ETC 50/VIII underwing bomb racks. The aircraft has a replacement rudder taken from an aircraft that was painted in a two tone camouflage pattern. Its radio code, T1+CH, identifies it as having been assigned to 1.(H)10. (Fraunhoffer)

A senior Army officer boards an Fw 189A of 11.(H)12 for a courier flight. In addition to its reconnaissance mission, the Fw 189 was also used for liaison and VIP transportation missions. (Fraunhoffer)

An Fw 189 of 2.(H)21 on the Russian plains during the Summer of 1943. The unit marking is carried on the outboard portion of the engine cowling and the aircraft carries Yellow bands on the tail booms. The S in the radio code was Red with a thin White outline. (Thiele)

Group	Squadron	Front Sector
NAG 8...	3.(H)13	North
	4.(H)23	"
	4.(FT)31	"
NAG 9...	1.(H)21	South
	7.(H)32	"
NAG 10.......................................	2.(H)10	Middle
	2.(H)31	"
	5.(H)32	"
NAG 11.......................................	1.(H)13	North
	1.(H) 31	"
NAG 12.......................................	6.(H)41	South
NAG 13.......................................	2.(H)21	"
	3.(H)41	"
NAG 15.......................................	1.(H)12	Middle
	6.(H)32	"
NAG 16.......................................	3.(H)12	South
	5.(H)12	"

The mission of the short-range. reconnaissance units became more and more dangerous as the Soviet offensive gained strength. In some units, observers were retrained as pilots so that they could carry out missions in single seat reconnaissance aircraft. This shortened training cycle only led to larger losses of crews and aircraft.

In May of 1942, the German 17th Army and the lst Armored(Tank) Army counter-attacked and managed to surround most of Timoshenko's Army attacking from the South. This action gave the Germans some breathing space to replace losses and re-equip units.

In air combat, the structure of the Fw 189 was proven to be robust and able to withstand considerable battle damage. In one action on 19 May 1942, two MiG-3 fighters attacked a Fw 189 at 13,123 feet (4,000m) over the Taman peninsula. They shot out the port engine and scored hits on the wing/boom joint causing the engine to separate from the aircraft. The flight mechanic and radio-operator's weapons were also out of action. Luckily the fighters broke off and even though heavily damaged, the Fw 189 was able to return for a crash landing at a forward airfield. When they landed, the port landing gear collapsed causing still further damage to the wing. After installing a new engine and repairing the wing tip, the aircraft was returned to service.

The German 11th Army took possession of Kerson peninsula and occupied the whole Krim peninsula during July of 1942. Soviet forces withdrew towards Stalingrad, retreating from the German troops that had broken through at Rostow. The German 6th Army completely destroyed the 62nd Soviet Army and lst Tank Army in the wetlands of Kalatsh. On 15 August 15 *Generaloberst* Paulus started his attempt to occupy Stalingrad.

The Stalingrad campaign led to the loss of a number of Fw 189s. On 18 September 1942 , an Fw 189 of 6 (H)41, escorted by four Bf 109 fighters, was conducting an artillery spotting mission over Stalingrad when the German formation was attacked by Soviet fighters. The Fw 189 was hit by the fighter flown by Ivan Balyuk and tried to escape. The aircraft was hit by fire from the Soviet flight commander, Dold Mihaylik, causing the port wing to fail and the Fw 189 crashed, killing *Oberfeldwebel* Manfred Köhle and *Stabsfeldwebel* Friedrich Lesska. Another aircraft was lost on 19 November when it was attacked by a Soviet fighter which scored hits on the starboard wing setting it on fire. The aircraft rolled inverted and dove into the ground.

This partially stripped Fw 189A crashed near the Don River in Russia during the Summer of 1943. The rudders are missing, along with some of the canopy sections. The aircraft belonged to 3.(H)12Pz. (Author)

To make up for losses suffered on the Eastern Front, a number of long-range reconnaissance formations were converted to short-range reconnaissance units, including the following:

Group	Squadron
NAG 1	3.(H)31 (ex 3.(F)31)
NAG 3	3.(H)11 (ex 3.(F)11)
NAG 6	2.(H)33 (ex 2.(F)33)
NAG 16	4.(H)33 (ex 4.(F)33)

Short-range reconnaissance units lost of almost twenty-five percent of their aircraft and crews during the battle for Stalingrad. When the Soviets launched their offensive against the Germans at Stalingrad, they committed their 2nd, 8th, 16th and 17th Air Armies against the dwindling Luftwaffe forces. In the first days of Soviet attack, Red Army armored forces overran the German forward airfields so quickly that the aircraft deployed there had little time to take off and some were destroyed on the ground. In spite of the odds, Fw 189s of the short-range reconnaissance units took off over and over again to support the surrounded 6th German Army. The air battles over Stalingrad and the surrounding area were heavy and fierce. On 17 December 1942, a Fw 189 spotting for German artillery was intercepted by a Soviet fighter flown by Dold Mihaylik. Flying at low altitude, the Fw 189 presented a difficult target for the Soviet fighter, but he finally was able to score hits on the tail plane causing the Fw 189 P2+BH of *Nahaufklärergruppe* 9 to crash. At the same time, another Fw 189, 5H+KK, of NAG 16, appeared above Davidovka, accompanied by Bf 109 fighters. The reconnaissance aircraft was attacked by Ivan Maximenko and his wingman Tchumbarev. Tchumbarev attacked the German formation but ran out of ammunition. Determined to destroy the Fw 189,

An Fw 189 of 1.(H)41 prepares to depart on another mission after being serviced on a Russian landing field. The aircraft carries Yellow bands on the tail booms and the wingtip outboard of the national marking is also Yellow. These Yellow markings were recognition markings applied to aircraft operating on the Eastern Front. (Petrick)

he rammed the Focke Wulf, cutting off the tail plane of the German aircraft with his propeller. The aircraft went out of control and the crew, *Oberfeldwebel* Mayer, *Unteroffizier* Schmidt and *Gefreiter* Sowa successfully bailed out although they were injured.

As of 2 February 1943, the Luftwaffe had lost 488 aircraft and 1,000 air crews in the region.

Ground crewmen refuel an Fw 189 for another reconnaissance mission on a grass landing ground in Russia during the Summer of 1943.

Hungarian troops pose with a damaged Fw 189 of 3.(H)12Pz near the Don River in Russia during the Summer of 1943. THe unit emblem was a Raven and was chosen to reflect the name of the unit's commander, *Oberleutnant* Raabe (Raven). (Author)

Ground crewmen load 110 pound (50 KG) anti-personnel bombs onto the ETC 50/VIII underwing bomb racks on an Fw 189A-1. These bombs were used against Russian partisans and other unarmored targets. (Szentpétery)

ETC 50/VIII Bomb Rack

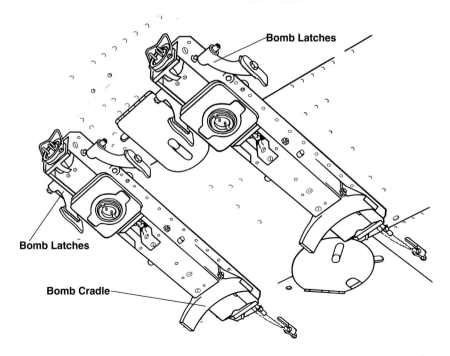

Bomb Latches

Bomb Latches

Bomb Cradle

The short-range reconnaissance units had lost some 150 aircraft, most of them Fw 189s. The newly established 3.(H)11 of NAG 3 lost six aircraft, Wr. Nr. 0206, Wr. Nr. 0147,Wr. Nr. 0240, Wr. Nr. 2307, Wr. Nr. 4212 and Wr. Nr. 2206 on 31 December 1942.

After Stalingrad, the Wehrmacht was in permanent retreat. There were some successful operations and during this time there was another reorganization of the Fw 189 units. Some units were given new identification numbers, including: 1.10 (ex 1.(H)10-1 of NAG12, 2.10 (ex NAG 9), 4.10 (ex 1.NAG 2 re-equipped with Bf 109s), 1.11(ex NAG 5) and 5.11(ex NAG 1). Several units were converted to other aircraft including a number of units which were retrained on reconnaissance variants of the Bf 110. In Caucasus, 1.21 continued to fly the Fw 189 along with 11.12(ex 1.(H)12) which was assigned to the middle section of the German front-line. NAG 2, 3, 5, 8 and 10 remained further back and began conversion training for either Bf 109 or Fw 190 A3/A4s.

The short-range reconnaissance forces were being ground down by the increasing strength of Soviet fighter units. Combat took place more often and Soviet ground based air defense units began to also improve, both in numbers and in accuracy. By 1943, a Fw 189 crew could expect getting at least one hit from Soviet ground fire on ninety percent of their missions.

From May of 1943 onward, the Fw 189s were used to engage Soviet partisans behind the front lines, using their relative slow flying speed. Despite the excellent Soviet camouflage, the Fw 189s were able to destroy large amounts of stores, staging areas and partisan camp sites .

In June of 1943, Operation CITADEL was begun in area around the Kursk salient. German reconnaissance aircraft were continuously in the air to observe the deployment of Soviet

This Fw 189A-1 of 1.(H)32 carried a camouflage of Dark Green and Olive Brown which was better suited to the Russian country-side along the northern portion of the Eastern Front than the standard German splinter camouflage schemes. (Fraunhoffer)

forces and their movements. Yak fighters of the French Normandie-Neman unit took part in the fighting and two French pilots, Lefevre and La Poype intercepted a Fw 189 and shot it down. Three days later Littolf and Castelain reported shooting down a twin fuselage aircraft above Marinka. LTs Marcel Albert and Albert Préziosi also attacked a reconnaissance aircraft above Brusna-Mekovaya on 16 June, destroying the aircraft. The German attack stopped at Harkov on 12 July and the Soviet counter-attack began at Orel. Fw 189 reconnaissance flights reported all of the Soviet movements of troops in time, but the Germans had no reserves to defend against these advances.

Two days later, Belgorod surrendered and five Soviet Armies began to move forward. The Soviet Air Force also deployed several new fighters including the Lavochkin La-5 which resembled the Fw 190 and caused recognition problems for the Fw 189 crews. Fw 189s tried to get through the front-line by flying at very low altitude, but the sheer numbers of Soviet fighters and anti-aircraft guns halted the entire German reconnaissance effort for extended periods.

During the Soviet Summer offensive, the Soviet Air Force deployed yet another new fighter, the Yak-3. With the introduction of this excellent low level fighter, Fw 189 operations would require additional fighter escorts. At this time, Fw 189s began to undertake night reconnaissance missions and had special equipment installed to allow them to operate at night or in bad weather. They continued to conduct only visual reconnaissance and rarely deployed photo flash bombs, as these would betray their positions to enemy gunners. As of 10 April 1944, *Luftflotte* 6 reported that the following units were equipped with Fw 189s: NAGr.4 (eight Fw

(Left) Luftwaffe ground crewmen refuel an Fw 189A-1 on the Eastern Front during 1943. Each tail boom of the Fw 189 contained a 29 gallon (110 L) fuel tank with the filler vent just over the wing. The bulges on the wing were maintenance access panels for the main wing attachment points.

Fw 189s of 1.(H)32 on the northern portion of the Eastern Front, either in or near Finland, carried a non-standard camouflage. This aircraft was armed with four 110 pound (50 kg) bombs on the underwing ETC bomb racks. (Fraunhoffer)

189s), NAGr.10 (twelve Fw 189s), NAGr.15 (fifteen Fw 189s) and 4.(H)31 (seven Fw 189s). Additionally, there were two aircraft assigned to I./NJG 100.

From the Summer of 1944 on, the Focke Wulf Fw 189 could not be used in the tactical reconnaissance role, even with strong fighter escorts since the aircraft were considered high priority targets for enemy fighters. Fw 189s were also used in the propaganda war. They took large numbers of handbills into action and on one mission a radio-operator downed a Soviet fighter by releasing a white cloud of handbills causing the pilot to loose control and crash.

The Fw 189s used for night flights remained in service during the Summer of 1944. Some units now operated a mix of aircraft and several flew Fw 189s, along with Bf 109Gs, Fw 190A-4s and Bf 110Cs.

In Finland, *Fliegerführer Nord(Ost)* of *Luftflotte 5* was engaged in heavy action. Among the 201 Luftwaffe aircraft in Finland, were seven Fw 189s of 1.(H)32 stationed at Kemijärvi, Alakurtti and Petsamo. These aircraft participated in reconnaissance missions along the Murmansk railway line, along with conducting support missions, including bombing missions and leaflet drops all along the front-line. During the first weeks of May, the unit lost a Fw 189 in a take-off accident. In June, the aircraft of 1.(H)32 were engaged in secret missions for XX Army Luftflotten-Verbindung.

In January of 1944 the unit settled into the airfield at Idriza, along with units of Luftflotte 1 including Stab/NAGr.5 and 1/NAGr.5, while 2/NAGr 5 was based at Petseri for a short time. 1.(H)32 at Petsamo lost one of their aircraft in combat near Alakurtti on 15 April, but the remaining aircraft of the unit flew some 1,000 sorties by 26 April 1944. On 12 May, another Fw 189 was lost to Soviet fighters in the Alakurtti area.

(Right) A Luftwaffe maintenance technician loads a film magazine for the RB20/30 aerial reconnaissance camera into a Fw 189A on the Eastern Front during 1943. The Fw 189 could carry an RB 20/30, RB 50/30, RB 21/18 or RB 15/18 camera in the center fuselage camera bay. Camera operation and control of picture interval and overlap were done by the observer/navigator.

An Fw 189A-1 of 121.(H)12 in Russia during 1943. The aircraft carried White tail boom stripes with Yellow underwing markings. The unit insignia was carried on both outboard engine cowlings. (Fraunhoffer)

An Fw 189A flys in trail with another Fw 189 over the Russian country side. Normally, Fw 189s flew at low level to avoid enemy fighters. The aircraft actually presented a rather difficult target for attacking fighters and could put up a surprising amount of defensive fire. (Petrick)

This Fw 189 was forced down due to fuel starvation near Tim, not far from the Don River in Russia. The fate of the crew is unknown. (Crecridlovsky)

In June, Fw 189 were still carrying out short-range reconnaissance tasks and three months later the Luftwaffe reported the following aircraft and units operating in Finland:

Base	Unit	Number of aircraft
Petsamo	1.(H)32	2
Alakurtti	"	2
Pontsalenjoki	"	3

All Luftwaffe activity officially ceased Finland on 15 September 1944.

This Fw 189 of 2.(H)31 made a forced landing during which the landing gear failed. In the resulting crash, the fuselage broke just forward of the wing. At the time of the crash both engines were still running and both wooden propellers were shattered when they came in contact with the ground. (Fraunhoffer)

This Fw 189A-1 of 3.(H) Pz/12 was stationed in the Don River area of the Eastern Front during the Summer of 1943.

This unusually camouflaged Fw 189A-1 of 1.(H) 32 was stationed on the Northern Front during 1942. This type of camouflage was only used in the Finnish area of operations.

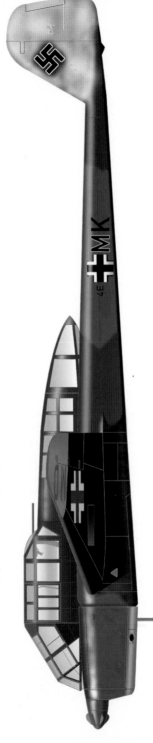

This Fw 189A-1 of 2.(H) 13 has the fin painted in Whitewash while the undersurfaces were in Black as a night camouflage.

An Fw 189A-1 of 11.(H) 12. The aircraft carries only a single letter code instead of the more usual four letter radio code on the fuselage side.

This Fw 189A-1 carries a winter camouflage of Whitewashed uppersurfaces over Light Blue undersurfaces.

This Fw 189A-1 of 1.(H) 31 has a Whitewash applied over the standard camouflage, including the unit insignia. The original camouflage was beginning to show through.

5D+KH

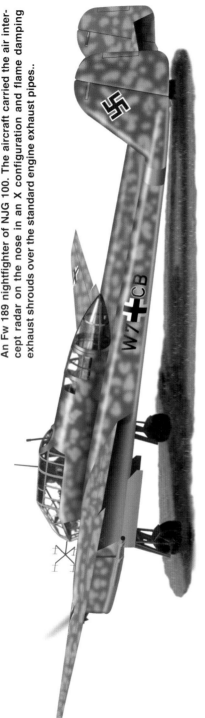

An Fw 189 nightfighter of NJG 100. The aircraft carried the air intercept radar on the nose in an X configuration and flame damping exhaust shrouds over the standard engine exhaust pipes..

W7+CB

Although assigned to 3/1 Squadron, Hungarian Air Force this Fw 189A-1 still carried full Luftwaffe camouflage and markings.

PC+LF

This Fw 189A-1 of 3/1 Squadron, Hungarian Air Force was named *HABLEÁNYKA* (Sirene).

Hableányka

F0+55

This Hungarian Air Force FW 189A-1 carries non-standard Hungarian national markings on the fuselage and wings.

BG+GK

The rear gunner on this Fw 189A-1 mans a single MG 15 7.9ᴍᴍ machine gun. The Fw 189 variants carried a variety of machine guns including the MG 81Z twin 7.9ᴍᴍ mount and single MG 81 machine gun mounts. These guns could be either drum fed or belt fed depending on the model being used.

Machine Guns

MG 15

MG 81

MG 81Z

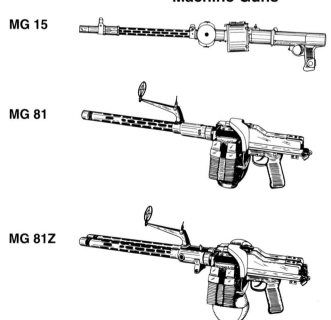

This Fw 189A-1 carries the unit insignia of 1.(H)31 on the cowling. The letter F in the radio code, 5D+FH, had a thin White outline. (Petrick)

A Luftwaffe ground crewman turns the inertial starter hand crank on an Fw 189A-1 of 11.(H)12 as another crewman in the cockpit prepares to start the port engine. The air-cooled Argus engines were easy to maintain and were reliable, an important feature, especially in the harsh Russian winter. (Fraunhoffer)

Ground crewmen make adjustments to the starboard engine of an Fw 189 of 5.(H)12 as it prepares for another reconnaissance mission over Russia. The E of the radio code, H1+EN, has a thin White outline The unit insignia was carried on the outboard engine cowling and consisted of a figure climbing a rope and blowing a horn. (Petrick)

Although this appears to be a desert type camouflage, this Fw 189A-1 was stationed in Russia. The aircraft carried the radio code SI+FG on the tail booms in Black. This type of camouflage was often called a "Worm" scheme by Luftwaffe personnel.(Kovács)

T1+EH an Fw 189A-1 of 5. (H)12 did not carry the unit insignia on the starboard outboard engine cowling. This is an early aircraft with single MG 15 machine guns in both the upper turret and tail cone position.

The colors of this "Worm" scheme were Sand Yellow over a Medium Green base on th uppersurfaces with Light Blue undersurfaces. This aircraft appears have just come from the paint shop since it does not have any theater identification markings and its defensive weapons had not yet been reinstalled. (Kovács)

Ground crews had a difficult time keeping the snow and ice off the aircraft and preparing them for action during the Russian winter. Protective covers were used to protect the cockpit and engines. Performing maintenance in the open under these conditions was a demanding task. (Kovács)

A ground crewman prepares to load an RB 50/30 aerial camera into an Fw 189A-1 at the start of another reconnaissance mission. In Russia, the severe winter cold made it necessary to wait until the last minute before loading the camera, since long exposure to the cold would damage the film. (Sinka)

A halftrack vehicle is used to tow this Fw 189 to its assigned parking sport through the deep snow on a Russian airfield. This aircraft is equipped with underwing ETC bomb racks.(Kovács)

An Fw 189A-1 shares a snow covered Russian airfield with an Heinkel He 46. The Fw 189 does not carry the standard Yellow Eastern Front identification bands on the tail booms. The fact that the aircraft is open and there are no covers on the engines would indicate that it is being readied for a mission. (Hefner)

This Fw 189 was severely damaged on a forward airfield in Russia. It was so badly damaged in the crash landing that it was written off and ground crews used it as a source of spare parts for other undamaged Fw 189s. (Petrick)

Armament crews load 110 pound (50 kg) bombs onto the ETC bomb racks of an Fw 189 on a snow covered airfield in Russia. These SC 50 bombs were equipped with streamers on the tail fins that produced a high pitched whistle when they fell.

This Fw 189 (4E+TK) was destroyed as a result of an engine fire and crash landing. Mechanics has already removed the armament from the wings and are in the process of removing other usable parts. (Petrick)

A ground crewmen removes the protective cover from the propeller spinner of an Fw 189 in Russia. These covers were necessary to protect the engines from the extreme cold. The Fw 189 was better suited to these conditions because of its air-cooled engines. Liquid cooled engines had to be pre-heated before they could be started.

This Fw 189A-1 of 1.(H) 31 carries the radio code 5D+KH. The aircraft has been winter camouflaged with Whitewash, but the ground crews were careful not to overpaint the radio code or swastika on the fin. (Matthiesen)

The winter Whitewash camouflage on this Fw 189A-1 was applied to the starboard side only and did not cover the Yellow Eastern Front identification bands on the tail booms. (Matthiesen)

This Fw 189A-1 was a new arrival on the Eastern Front during the Winter of 1943/44 and did not have the Yellow Eastern Front identification markings. SI+EG is an early Fw 189A-1 with a single MG 15 7.9MM machine gun in the upper turret. The aircraft in the background is a Junkers W 34. The large radio direction finder loop antenna on the upper fuselage indicates that this aircraft was used as an airborne radio operator training aircraft. (Hefner)

An Fw 189 splashes across a slushy Russian airfield at Rostow during January of 1943. The aircraft was unusual in that the spinners were different colors. The aircraft in the background is an Fw 190 fighter. (Petrick)

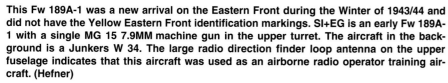

(Left) This winter Whitewashed Fw 189A-2 was equipped with an MG 81Z twin 7.9mm machine gun mount in an armored glass upper turret. The aircraft has had the radio code partially overpainted with temporary winter Whitewash camouflage, although the P with its White outline clearly shows through. The swastika insignia on the fin is of an unusual style. The Whitewash was applied to the upper-surfaces and fuselage/tail boom sides only. The undersurfaces remained the standard Light Blue (RLM 65). (Kovács)

(Below/left) Armament crews load an SC 50 bomb onto the ETC bomb rack of an Fw 189 of 2.(H)31. The unit's winged tank insignia was carried on the outboard cowing pane and consisted of a Black tank with White wings on a Red background with a Blue outline. (Fraunhoffer)

(Below) This Fw 189A-2 had the starboard main landing gear break through the ice on a forward airfield in Russia during the Winter of 1943/44. The aircraft carries a highly weathered temporary winter Whitewash camouflage on the uppersurfaces. The aircraft is equipped with the late style MG 81Z twin gun rear turret with its external shell casing ejection chute under the rear fuselage.

The crew of this Fw 189A-2 prepares to deplane after another mission over Russia. The The gunner appears to be securing an access panel on the aircraft while the pilot waits for him.

(Above) An Fw 189A warms up its engines before departing on a reconnaissance mission. The aircraft has been given a temporary winter camouflage of Whitewash applied to the aircraft's uppersurfaces directly over the standard camouflage finish (except for the cockpit area).This finish did not weather well and the standard finish is beginning to wear through on the engine cowling.

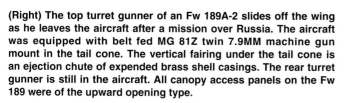

(Right) The top turret gunner of an Fw 189A-2 slides off the wing as he leaves the aircraft after a mission over Russia. The aircraft was equipped with belt fed MG 81Z twin 7.9MM machine gun mount in the tail cone. The vertical fairing under the tail cone is an ejection chute of expended brass shell casings. The rear turret gunner is still in the aircraft. All canopy access panels on the Fw 189 were of the upward opening type.

This Fw 189 of 2.(H)13 had the uppersurfaces given a Whitewash finish and carried the radio code 4E+MK. The aircraft was unusual in that it had dark colored undersurfaces. Most Fw 189s were painted with a Light Blue on the undersurfaces. (Petrick)

Luftwaffe armament crews prepare to load belted 7.9ᴍᴍ machine gun ammunition into the ammunition storage bins in the rear turret of a Whitewashed Fw 189 on the Eastern Front.

A belt fed MG 81Z twin gun mount in the rear turret of an Fw 189A-2. This gun had a high rate of fire, although it was hampered by its relatively small bore. (Thiele)

An armament crew load AB 250 weapons carriers onto the ETC bomb racks of an FW 189. The weapons carrier could be loaded with a variety of loads such as SD-2 Butterfly anti-personnel bomblets. (Sinka)

The ETC 50/VIII bomb rack had one locking lug near the front of the rack (the small circle) which engaged the eye bolt on the bomb. Once the bomb is secured in place, the forward latches were move down to help hold the bomb in place.

Armament crews load what appear to be supply canisters onto the wing bomb racks of an Fw 189 on the Eastern Front. The aircraft has an unusual Whitewash camouflage pattern which left large areas of the base color show through.

Ground crewmen prepare to refuel an Fw 189 on a snow covered Russian airfield. the two small air intakes on either side of the main engine air intake fed cooling air into the oil cooler trunking. While some Fw 189s had an radio antenna above the cabin, all had this radio antenna mast below the fuselage.

An Fw 189A-1 flies close formation with another Fw 189. The aircraft carries the standard splinter type camouflage and theater identification bands on the tail booms. (Author)

The observer (left) and pilot of an Fw 189. There is an anti-glare sunshield installed above them to allow for a better view of the terrain below the aircraft. The two striped tubes looped around in the nose are the brake lines for the main landing gear. (Szentpéteri)

Using a model as a training aid, a gunner describes the cones of fire of the defensive gun positions on an Fw 189A-2. There is a jack placed under the fuselage to hold the aircraft as ground crews work on the port landing gear. (Author)

An Fw 189A-1 on the airfield at Kharkov, in the Ukraine during early 1943. The Balkenkreuz national insignia on the tail boom overlaps into the theater identification band and the radio codes have been painted out. (Author)

This Fw 189A-1 was assigned to 6.(H)13 in the middle sector of the Eastern Front. (Petrick)

An Fw 189A-1 (BF+HJ) flies formation with an Ju 87D-3 Stuka. The Fw 189 was configured with ETC bomb racks and had an unusual Eastern Front theater marking under the wing. The Yellow underwing marking extends from the wingtip all the way back to the end of the aileron. The J of the radio code is carried in this area in Black. (Fraunhoffer)

Fw 189As assigned to training units carried large identification numbers in White on the fin. This Fw 189, White 109, also carried the radio identification code KC+JN. The aircraft was assigned to a Ju 88 bomber training unit located on the Baltic Sea during 1944. (Author)

Ground crewmen perform routine checks on an Fw 189 of 2.(H)13 during the Winter of 1942. This aircraft has had the undersides painted in Black for the night reconnaissance role. (Petrick)

This Fw 189A-2 was guided up to a special parking spot for ceremonies marking the unit's 4,000th sortie. The aircraft is unusual in that is has different colored spinners and a flash hider on the MG 17 wing gun. (Petrick)

This aircraft carries a wreath on the nose to celebrate the unit's 2,000 sortie. The Fw 189A-2 has a White Swan marking below the cockpit canopy. (Fraunhoffer)

Nightfighters

During 1944, a number of Fw 189A-1s were modified as auxiliary night fighter aircraft. An FuG 212C-1 Litchenstein airborne intercept radar was installed in the nose and a 20MM MG151/15 or MG151/20 was mounted in the fuselage fixed to fire upward at angle. These aircraft were called Behelfsnachtjöger (auxiliary night-fighters) and were used in combat mostly over the Eastern front against slow and low flying Soviet night intruder aircraft.

An Fw 189 Nightfighter of NJG 100. The Fw 189A-1 nightfighter was modified with an FuG212C-1 airborne intercept radar antenna on the nose, flame dampers on the exhausts and an upward firing MG 151 20MM cannon in place of the upper gun turret. (Birkholz)

Nightfighter Modifications

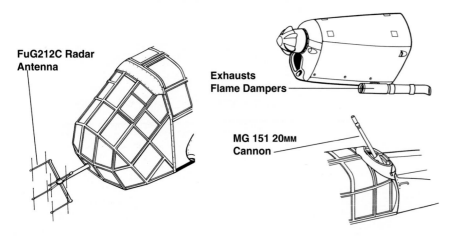

FuG212C Radar Antenna

Exhausts Flame Dampers

MG 151 20MM Cannon

38

Foreign Service

Slovakian Air Force

The German established Slovakian Air Force was equipped with modern German aircraft to be used on the Eastern Front against the Soviets. The Slovakian Air Force received a total of fourteen Fw 189A-1s to outfit a tactical reconnaissance squadron for service on the Eastern Front.

During 1942/43, this unit was in combat in the Krim area, but during the Slovakian uprising of the late Summer of 1944, the Slovakian flyers were ordered to return to their home air bases. On the airfield at Try Duby (Three Oaks), a number of aircraft had been gathered to support the insurgent forces, including several Fw 189s. German air superiority; however, quickly overcame this small force. The uprising was soon quelled and on 31 August 1944, the last six Fw 189s flew to the Soviet Union loaded with Slovakian fugitives.

(Right) This Slovakian Air Force Fw 189 carries the markings applied to aircraft of the Czech national uprising during the Summer of 1944. The aircraft was damaged and unable to fly out of Tri Duby (Three Oaks) during the evacuation to Poland and was destroyed on the field. (Zdenek Hurt via Hans-Heiri Stapfer)

An Fw 189A-2 of the Slovakian Air Force on an airfield near the Tatra mountains during 1944. The insignia consisted of a Blue cross with a Red circle superimposed in the center of the insignia and a White border. The Slovakian Air Force operated at least fourteen Fw 189A-2s. (via Hans-Heiri Stapfer)

Royal Romanian Air Force

The Fw 189 first entered service as a trainer to convert reconnaissance pilots from single engine into twin engine aircraft. Until the arrival of the Fw 189s, Romanian pilots had flown the IAR-29 and Hs 129. The first Fw 189s were put into service at Galac, where a flying school was set up. Operational training was completed at Kirovograd in the Soviet Union, where Grupu 8 Assault (.8th Battle Group) was stationed between May and August of 1944. These machines usually retained their original German camouflage scheme and radio codes.

In the Summer of 1944, the group began night flying training on the airfields at Arad (Oradea) and Tecuc. This training was conducted for crews selected to man night fighter and night reconnaissance aircraft. These plans were not to be put into action because on 23 August 1944, advancing troops found several abandoned Fw 189s on airfields deserted by the retreating German forces. These aircraft were later handed over to the Red Air Force.

Royal Bulgarian Air Force

The Bulgarian Air Force received a number of Fw 189As to re-equip their short range reconnaissance units. These aircraft saw action on the Russian Front during 1943 and carried the Cross of St Andrew on the fuselage in Black against a White background.

Royal Hungarian Air Force

During the Spring of 1943 it became obvious that the Hungarian short-range reconnaissance squadrons, which were equipped with Heinkel He 46 and Weiss Manfred W.M.21, were obsolete and in need of re-equipment. The German High Command decided that it was important to upgrade the allied air forces that were to serve along side Luftwaffe units.

This ex-Romanian Air Force Fw 189 was evaluated by the Soviets at Zhukovsky air base. The aircraft was repainted with Soviet stars on the fin and tail booms and the rudder was painted Yellow. (Gretzyngier).

White 14 was one of several Fw 189A-1s operated by the Royal Bulgarian Air Force on the Eastern Front. The aircraft carried the insignia adopted after Bulgaria joined the Axis and an "eye" unit insignia on the outboard cowling panel. (Marii Chernev)

The squadrons which were deployed in middle section of the Eastern Front were replaced by 3/l Magyar Királyi Honvéd Repülo Század (Royal Hungarian "Honvéd" Flyer Squadron), led by CAPT Loránd Telbisz. This squadron was under the operational control of *Luftflotte 4*. The unit was trained on the Fw 189 in Proskurov used German aircraft assigned to *Aufklärungsgruppe 3*. They received twelve Fw 189As during May of 1943. The crews gave the new aircraft the nickname "Bel'Ami" after a German movie star.

The Fw 189s deployed to the airfield at Harkov South on 18 May. Two aircraft were further deployed to the area around the Pripjet marsh for use against Russian partisans. One of these aircraft was shot down on 22 May. The unit flew a total of 224 sorties before being thrust into the Battle of Kursk. The area in front of the Hungarian lines was 74.5 miles (120 km) long and

Hungarian aircrews were trained on the Fw 189A-1 at Proshkurov airfield in the Ukraine during 1943. Although assigned to the Hungarian Air Force, these Fw 189s carried Luftwaffe markings. (Suttay)

This "worm" camouflaged Fw 189, radio code PC+LF was flown by an Hungarian crew commanded by SGT Endre Czigány. (Czigány)

These Hungarian crewmen, CAPT Vetö (KIA), 2LT Székely (captured) and SGT Lakovics (wounded) were the first Hungarian crew to be lost in combat. The aircraft was shot down by ground fire on 23 May 1943. (Székely)

A Hungarian Air Force Fw 189 with the Pegasus emblem on the outboard cowling panel in White. The Pegasus was the unit insignia for 3/1 Squadron, Royal Hungarian Air Force. (Author)

25-30 miles (40-50 km) wide. During the battle, the Hungarian Fw 189s were also used for low altitude bombing missions as well as forward reconnaissance. With the Soviet break-through, all units of the Hungarian air force was withdrawn.

On 21 September 1943, three Yak 9s attacked Cornet Béla Csapó and his crew north of Kiev. The Fw 189 dove to low altitude and its gunner managed to shoot down one of the Soviet fighters, while another hit the ground trying to follow the twisting and turning Fw 189. The last Yak 9 broke off the engagement and flew off. On that same day, six Lavotchkin La-5s attacked Sergeant János Suttay's aircraft. The crew shot down two of the fighters and managed to escape back to friendly territory.

By the end of October, the Hungarian unit recorded its 1,000th sortie. And until the end of the year, the unit was in constant action. The number of combat sorties was reduced; however, because of a lack of operational aircraft. Between May and December, some sixty aircraft had received battle damage, mainly from Soviet ground fire, although another twelve had been damaged by enemy fighters. By the time the unit moved back into Hungary in March of 1944, it had only one operational aircraft remaining and 3/1 Squadron was disbanded. .

On 1 April 1944, the 4/l Short-range Reconnaissance Squadron arrived from Hungary at Bromberg (Bydgosc) led by CAPT József Fraunhoffer. This squadron was trained in night fly-ing and instrument flight under poor weather conditions. The unit was known as the ***Erweiterte Atifklärer Ausbildung*** and was to be used in the "twilight" reconnaissance role. On 18 May, their training was completed and they began operations (some missions had

already been flown while still in training) The unit's area of operations was between Delatin and Kolomea. In early April, they flew to Zamosc in Poland to support the 1st Hungarian Army. This action resulted in high losses. Their last operational move was to Ungvar(Ushgorod in Russia) and from there they transferred to Gödölló, near Budapest in September. Here they handed over their aircraft to the Germans. During their operational career, the squadron had lost ten-eleven aircraft, five to Soviet fighters and one to an operational accident (weather), the rest were to ground fire.

During the last few months of the war, Hungarian Air Force short-range reconnaissance forces were undergoing conversion training for the Messerschmitt Bf 109, but the war ended before this was complete.

(Left) SGT Ferenc Nyakas points to the name on the tail boom of his Fw 189. The aircraft was named *Pintyöke* (Finch). (Suttay)

A Hungarian crewmen in the rear gunners station of an Fw 189. There were differences in the crew makeup between German and Hungarian Fw 189 crews. In the Hungarian Air Force, the rear gunner also doubled as the radio operator. In the Luftwaffe, the observer doubled as radio operator. (Author)

This Fw 189 carried non-standard national markings on the tail boom. Normally the Hungarian insignia did not extend to the edges of the Black box. The aircraft carried the name *Hableányka* (Sirene) on the port boom in White and the name *Ica* (Helen) in the same position on the starboard boom. (Suttay)

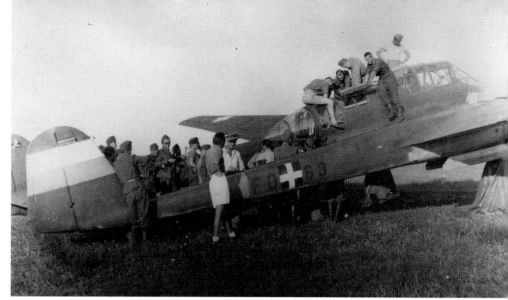

Crews crowd around a newly arrived Fw 189A-1 with the radio code FO+63. The national markings on the fin consisted of (top to bottom) bands of Red, White, Green. The wing and boom markings consisted of a White cross on a Black square. (Suttay)

Crews of the 3/1 Squadron, Royal Hungarian Air Force pose with one of their Fw 189s when the unit achieved its 1,000 sortie in October of 1943. At the time the unit was stationed at Sitikovka in the Ukraine and was commanded by CAPT Telbisz (center/standing). (Author)

The Fw 189 was a strong aircraft. This Hungarian Fw 189 has had the entire vertical fin in front of the rudder shot way by Russian anti-aircraft fire. In spite of this damage, the aircraft made it safely back to base. (Czigány)

Ground crewmen work to replace the entire vertical tail section of SGT Czigány's Fw 189 after it was shot way by Soviet ground fire. (Czigány)

43

(Left) A Royal Hungarian Air Force Fw 189 flies formation with a Luftwaffe Fw 189 over the Eastern Front. Such flights were rare, since most Fw 189 reconnaissance missions were flown solo, or at most with a fighter escort. The MG 15 in the upper turret was fitted with a sun shield over the sights. This upper turret gun was fitted with a variety of different types of gun sights and it was not unusual for aircraft within the same unit to be configured differently. (Czigány)

1LT Gombos (left) and his observer refer to the map of the area they are to cover. The circle in front of 1LT Gombos is the gun sight for the two forward firing MG 17 7.9ᴍᴍ machine guns. The flight instruments were located on the panel in front of and above the pilot's head. (Gombos)

Hungarian air crewmen survey the SC 50 110 pound (50kg) bombs that are to be loaded onto their Fw 189A-1. These bombs were fitted with streamers attached to the tail fins. These would deploy when the bomb was dropped setting up a whistle that could be heard for miles. The small ring on the bomb was the attachment lug which locked the bomb into the ETC 50/VII bomb rack. (Csapó)

1LT Gombos of 3/1 Squadron poses in the cockpit opening of his Fw 189 during a lull in operations on the Eastern Front during 1943. During his operational career flying for the Royal Hungarian Air Force, he was attacked on three separate occasions by Soviet fighters. (Gombos)

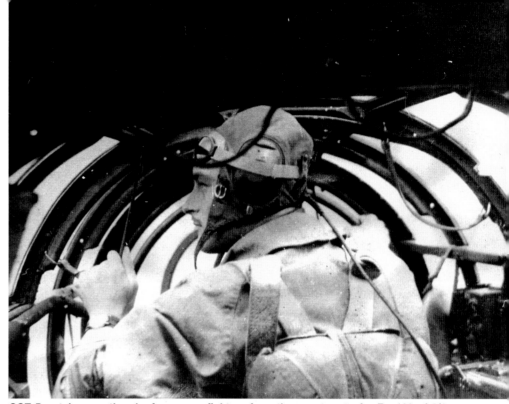

SGT Pusztai scans the sky for enemy fighters from the rear turret of a Fw 189 of 3/1 Squadron, Royal Hungarian Air Force. The two belts hanging from the fuselage roof were hand holds intended to assist the gunner in operating his turret. (Pusztai)

Ground crews rest near an Fw 189 of 3/1 Squadron. The aircraft still carries a German radio code, BG+ZJ and has the Eastern Front tail boom Yellow band much further back on the boom than normal. Additionally, the aircraft has an unpainted starboard engine cowling, probably a replacement for a damaged engine. (Gombos)

Hungarian crews use the horizontal stabilizer of this freshly repainted Fw 189A-2 of 3/1 Squadron to hold a debriefing session. During this time period, the squadron was operating from Kharkov South Airfield in the Ukraine. (Suttay)

The wing mounted MG 17 machine gun has been removed from this Hungarian Fw 189 and the gun port has been faired over. The tube extending down from under the center fuselage section was used to drop weighted message streamers to ground troops. (Author)

This Hungarian Fw 189 has not yet been repainted with Royal Hungarian Air Force wing marking and still has German insignia on the upper wing. This is an early production Fw 189A-1 with the single MG 81 upper turret. The gun has been outfitted with a sun shield over the gun sight. (Gyulay)

Ground and air crews rest alongside an old Fw 189A-1 that was issued to the newly formed 4/1 Squadron, Royal Hungarian Air Force at its home base in Poland during early 1944. (Gombos)

Reconnaissance missions over Soviet territory were often flown alone and unescorted. That made the Fw 189s easy targets for fighters. This Fw 189 took a hit in the rudder from a fighter cannon shell which exploded on impact. Even with this degree of damage, the aircraft made it safely back to base. (Suttay)

In addition to the damaged rudder, shell fragments also tore holes in the vertical stabilizer and tail boom. Reportedly, the rudder was scrapped and replaced with one from another damaged Fw 189. The fin colors were (top-bottom) Red, White, Green. (Suttay)

(Right) An Fw 189A-1 of 3/1 Squadron, Royal Hungarian Air Force on a reconnaissance mission over Russia during 1943. The aircraft has a bare metal propeller spinner on the port engine which indicates that it was a recent replacement that the ground crews have not had time to paint. The MG 81 in the upper turret was fitted with a sun shield over the gun sight. .(Czigány).

47

This Hungarian Fw 189A-1 ran out of fuel and was forced to land at Gotzkau on 19 May 1944 where it drew a crowd of civilians. The aircraft was painted with Light Gray uppersurfaces over Light Blue undersurfaces. (Szalóki)

The ground crewmen under this Fw 189A-1, radio code BG+GK, is preparing packets of leaflets to be loaded into the aircraft for a leaflet dropping mission over Soviet lines. The insignia on the tail boom consists of the old German marking overpainted with White. (Gombos)

This Fw 189 was severely damaged by Soviet anti-aircraft fire while on a mission over the Eastern Front during 1944. The rudder, vertical stabilizer, elevator and horizontal stabilizer have all suffered battle damage. (Author)

A Hungarian Air Force pilot in the cockpit of his Fw 189A-1. The flight instruments are on a panel just in front and above his head. There is also a folding anti-glare panel installed in the nose just in front of the pilot to make the take off a little safer. (Gombos)

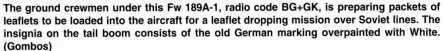

Last Flights

Focke Wulf Fw 189 aircraft remained in training units and some were used for liaison missions up until the end of the war. The last Luftwaffe Fw 189 losses were reported by Stab I./NAGr.5 on 8 May 1945. The squadron reported that Fw 189A-2 Wr. Nr. 2274 (U2+ZB) and Fw 189A-2 Wr. Nr.125345 (U2+RB) were both flown to Bulltofta/Sweden on that date.

At least one Fw 189 was used as a hack by the Royal Flying Establishment in England after the war. After its usefulness had past, the aircraft was placed into storage at RAF Brize Norton. Unfortunately, the aircraft was later destroyed in a gale.

(Right) This was one of two Fw 189s from I./NAGr.5 that defected to Bulltofta, Sweden on 8 May 1945, the last two Fw 189 losses recorded by the Luftwaffe. The aircraft were stripped by local souvenir hunters (Kulikov via Hans-Heiri Stapfer)

This captured fw 189A-3 was evaluated by the Royal Air Force at the Royal Aircraft Establishment, Boscombe Down during the Fall of 1945. It was assigned the Air Ministry number 27 for these tests. After the aircraft had outlived its usefulness it was placed in storage, but was destroyed in a gale some time later. (Hans-Heiri Stapfer)

Luftwaffe Aircraft of the Second World War
from
squadron/signal publications

1030

1044

1057

1073

1085

1113